Serenity Symbols Coloring Book

Written and Illustrated by

Deborah Levine Herman

Soul Odyssey Media
Stockbridge, MA

Micro Publishing Media
PO Box 1522
Stockbridge, MA 01262
www.soulodysseybooks.com
micropublishingmedia@gmail.com

isbn: 978-1-936517-87-9

How to Use this Book:

These illustrations are done through a process I call automatic drawing. I hold the pen lightly and the energy does the rest. With the exception of the cover design, in which I incorporated some calculated drawing, each illustration is done with only one line. I like to use colored pencils to color the drawings but you should try anything you like.

Please have fun as you find the colors that are most pleasing to you. Reading the messages is only part of the experience. Don't be afraid to let go and remember the joy you felt as a child when given a new box of crayons and pencils. Be free to experience your own artistic voice.

May you be filled with serenity and peace as
you rediscover how much you are truly loved.

Blessings,

Deborah Herman

Feelings

There is nothing to fear as feelings are not facts. My feelings cannot harm me. Feelings can be memories that do not belong in the present. I use my feelings to learn about myself. They are my teachers. I will not block them numb them or bury them but will let them run their course. I bless my feelings and listen to them.

Serenity

I am free of all addictions. There is nothing I do without God at my side. When I feel the desire to hurt myself in any way through thought, deed or unkind words I turn inward and know that my prayers will be answered. I will be filled with strength and love. This is how I maintain my serenity.

Forgiveness

I do not blame others for my choices. All
humans are limited by the tools they are
given. Even the miss-takes I have made
have helped me find my way to God.
I no longer give power to those people
who have disappointed me or hurt me.
I now understand that most people do not
act against someone else but rather for
themselves. I am my own person.
I forgive others and I forgive myself.

Choose

At any moment I am free to choose a new
path regardless of past decisions. Many of
my choices were made without the clear
understanding of who I am and what I
want out of the gift of life I have been
given. If I am facing obstacles at every turn
I now look more closely to see if perhaps
I am holding on too tightly to a path
that is not suited to me. I speak honestly
to myself as I weigh my choices carefully.

Process

My life is a process. I understand that the
journey is as important as the destination.
I am not expected to know things before I
learn them. Sometimes I learn with great
difficulty and stubborness. When I am
true to myself I feel joyous and free. This is
when I am most connected to God. This is
when my process is easiest.
I have the courage to support my own
convictions and trust God to guide me back
to safety when I am facing a tough lesson.

Divine Spark

I am filled with the flame of my own Divine spark. I expect good things because God wants them for me. I deserve Health, happiness and love. I deserve unconditional love from myself and others. I do not judge myself harshly and give the same kindness to others.

This releases me from resentments and helps me reach wholeness. I recognize the Divine Spark in all others even if they do not recognize it in themselves.

Surrender

I can change my life with one thought:
I surrender!
I will no longer isolate myself
from others because of a mistaken belief
that I am unworthy or not good enough.
This is a falsehood. God knows
everything about me. I can believe
in God but now I know that God
believes in me.

Mirrors

I am a mirror for others as they are mirrors
for me. I allow my Divine light to shine
outward from my soul so that others may
see themselves as God sees them. With
this love and acceptance of others I know
they will reflect back to me that I too
am loved. We are all connected.

No Regrets

I am a perfect creation even though I am not perfect. I no longer become disappointed in myself when I fail to meet some false expectation. When I live in the moment I do not have the opportunity to criticize myself. I am not caught up in a cycle of comparison between some not yet lived future or some regret of the past. All things are as they should be in every moment.

Compassion

I understand the suffering of others. I allow myself to be a vessel of compassion and forgiveness even toward those I believe have hurt me. I understand that all people are wounded. My soul path is between me and God. I am strong and confident that if I follow my heart I will find the path that is right for me. I give compassion but allow others their path. I do not judge them nor do I take responsibility for their struggles.

Retreat

Fight or flight. When I am faced with life's challenges I may feel overwhelmed. I may feel nervous and have anxiety. What I no longer do is retreat or escape in ways that are not healthy for me.

When I feel frightened by the unknown or the obstacles in front of me I find ways to soothe myself. I take a walk. I sit in gratitude. I read or listen to music. I often treasure my time alone but if I am avoiding people I use this time to reach out. For all I know they are waiting for me to help them feel more connected.

Turbulance

There will always be turbulance as it is part of life. I can fearlessly face the unexpected as I have all the tools I need.
The random things that happen are not punishments. They are also not always random. If I am able to quiet my mind and observe my circumstances objectively I will find the messages that are meant to guide me.
Some days are simply difficult. I now fully understand that other people also have difficult days. I reach out to help when I can as helping others also helps me.

Infinite Love

I open my heart to love even if the love I give is not always returned. Loving takes nothing away from me as I have it in infinite supply. If my love is not returned in kind I look to God for my nourishment. Some people are unable to receive love without suspicion. I have compassion for people who put walls around their hearts. I no longer need to live that way as I do not fear love or the loss of love. I know Love is infinite.

Assumptions

I do not assume things about other people because I do not like it when people make assumptions about me. I am more than my afflictions. I am more than behaviors and choices. These are all parts of my journey to wholeness. I do not make assumptions about myself. If I have made choices in the past that do not suit me, this does not mean I will make the same choices in the future.

Stubborn

Each day I turn my life over to a power greater than myself. God as I understand God is at the center of my universe. This empowers me and aligns me with the Divine Spark that is within my soul. This is how I know God's will for me. It is always better than what I think I want for myself as I am often stubborn and lacking in confidence. When I am serene I know that my path is clear. I have learned to listen.

Gratitude

I have learned that my true happiness will only come from gratitude. When I fully understand the gift of life and the blessings available to me I am in charge of my serenity. No matter what kind of day I am having, when I remember to be grateful I return to my center point and find myself at peace.

Honor

I honor the parts of me that are
troublesome as I treasure the parts of me
that are healthy and serene. For if I had
no challenges, obstacles or character
flaws, I would never have the motivation to
change. There would be no reason for
compassion and no wisdom to be gained
from experience. I bless all the times I have
felt in darkness for those are the moments
that have led me to the light.

Honesty

I have the courage to be honest with
myself and others. I know now there is
nothing so awful about myself that I have
to hide it behind shame or blame. I forgive myself for misinterpreting the nature
of God.

I believed that I had to earn God's love and
that I would always fall short. There is
nothing I could ever think, say or do that
would cause God to lose faith in me. I now
have equal faith in myself. I am not afraid
to step into my own greatness.

I Quit

Sometimes I feel like quitting. It doesn't matter what I am doing, I feel I can't do it anymore. This is when I take a deep breath, relax and think about why I am feeling this way. Most of the time it is because of self-doubt. Am I good enough? Am I up to the task? I realize that I am holding myself up to impossible standards of perfection. If I am doing my best there is nothing more that I can do. What I will not do is quit. Even if I fail to meet what I believe others expect of me or the impossible perfection I expect, if I don't quit I am perfect.

Lost

When I miss my loved ones who are
far away or who have left the earth I often
feel that I am lost without their
guidance. I now know that they are but
a thought away. I also know that I have all
the answers I need within the confines of
my soul. This is where my serenity is
found.

Success

I am no longer afraid of success. I now accept that there are never really any lost opportunities if I was not yet ready to accept them. God is infinitely patient as I learn of my own greatness. I now know that true success is feeling comfortable in my own skin at any time and on any day no matter what is happening around me. I no longer compare myself to other people as I have no idea what their pain might be. I require enough work, love and self-compassion. I can't imagine the challenges of another. Nor would I trade my individual soul path for theirs.

Nature

The perfection of nature teaches me
that the universe makes no mistakes. I must
therefore never consider that I might be a
mistake. When I am feeling sorry for myself
or disconnected I remember the love that
must have gone into the creation of every
single creature, plant, stone and tree. With
this in mind I remember that there is a
grand design for everything and of this
I am a significant part.

Validation

I am ready to have other people in my life. I am learning to trust the right people and to choose friends and loved ones who add to the quality of my life as I hope to add to the quality of theirs. I do not need to maintain relationships with people who drain my energy without "seeing" me as God sees me.

When I see myself as God sees me I know that I am worthy of love and joy. I do not choose companionship with others who do not support my authentic self because of a false need for outside validation. I now validate myself.

Myself

I see myself in others. This is a good way to learn about myself. I am, however, not other people so I do not define myself through them.

If I am an observer I can have compassion and empathy without losing myself in other people's lessons and choices. By standing in my own light I am able to help others see the good in themselves. By standing in my own light I do not lose sight of myself.

Destiny

I know I have a destiny. There is a reason for me to be alive. This reason could be as simple as whatever I do in the next moment. I do not know how a simple smile or gesture can influence the path of myself or another. Therefore, I am not waiting for my life to begin in some distant future or for some distant goal. My life is right now, right in this moment. Now is my destiny and I know it is for a very good reason. I cherish every moment.

Stirrings

The stirrings in my heart sometimes tell me that everything is not okay. I am often restless and nervous like I have done something wrong but I do not know what it is. When I feel these types of stirrings I tell myself that everything is fine. Everything IS fine. If I am breathing there is nothing that with God's help I am unable to face. There is no problem that I can't solve. If something is too difficult for me perhaps it is telling me to go in a different direction. Rather than turning against myself I open to the stirrings of God who is always there for me.

Money

Money is energy. I am not afraid to have it and I am not afraid to not have it. I have faith that I will be given what I need if I ask for it with an open heart. This can mean having the guidance to find a job, or it can mean having gratitude when I am able to take care of myself financially . It can also mean having compassion for myself and others when we are unable to do so. I am not ashamed to ask and receive help when I need it. I am also willing to help others when it is I who is prosperous always understanding that there is always a short distance between having and having not.

Advice

I appreciate when people want to give me unsolicited advice. However, I know that I do not have to take it. Sometimes advice is good but sometimes it is the exercise of someone else's will. I am open to other points of view and do not need to do everything my own way. I give the greatest weight to my inner self and to my connection to God. I trust my soul more than I trust other people. I have the courage to believe I could be right even when faced with the strong opinions of others. If I make a miss-take it is my right to be wrong.

Rejection

It is sometimes easier to disquise my feelings by becoming the center of attention. If I act like I don't care I don't have to face the possibility of rejection. I do this by how I carry myself or by creating unnecessary drama. I have learned that if I simply ask for what I need people will typically give it to me. If I am rejected it does not become my self definition. I expend my energy on the people who will not reject me rather than trying to win the love of those who do not return it. We can't all be loved by everyone. We are all loved by God.

Hunger

Hunger can mean many things. I appreciate the physical sensation because it helps me to connect to the natural rhythms of my body. I answer its call appropriately with nourishment.

Sometimes hunger is really for love. These sensations are not so easy to distinguish. I am becoming more aware of when my emotional hunger sends its natural signals requesting appropriate nourishment. I heed this call by reaching out to others, allowing healthy relationships and giving love. I do not suppress emotional hunger by feeding it junk.

Alone

Sometimes I sit in a crowd and listen. I am alone yet I feel connected. Every person has a story to tell. I used to envy what I perceived as the happiness and carefree nature of others and my own loneliness. I now know that every person's story is filled with the same twists and turns as mine. I smile as I know I am never truly alone.

Soulmate

I have always wanted a soulmate but would set limits and expectations. Allowing God to choose the companion, partner or friend best for me assures that this person will reflect the highest part of me. Like attracts like. God knows my soul and my greatest self. Therefore I turn these choices over to God as I learn to become my greatest self. My greatest self is also my authentic self. When I am in full acceptance of who I am I will be a true reflection of God on Earth.

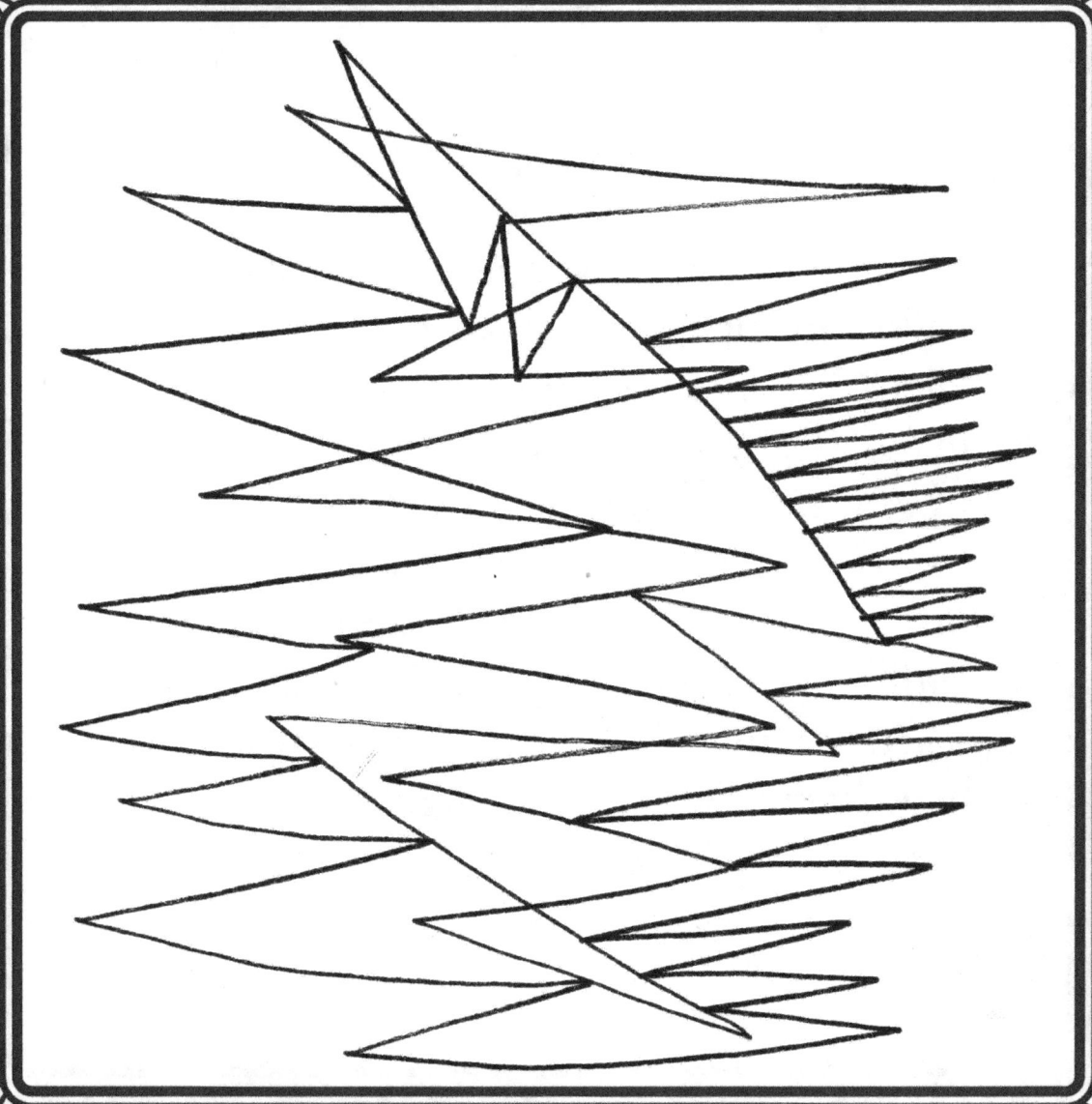

Moods

My moods change with my circumstances. If I allow the ups and downs of my life to dictate my moods I am a passive participant in my life. I recognize my moods as separate from my circumstances so I can regulate them accordingly. Negativity will influence my circumstances so I maintain a positive attitude whenever possible. There are times when the only thing I can truly control is how I view things. My thoughts are completely my own.

Age

Life is a continuum. When my body is young I treat it well so it will be healthy in my future. I do not resent or resist age in myself or others but rather appreciate the passage of time for the experience it affords me.

I respect those younger than me for their enthusiasm and fresh point of view. I respect those older than me for their wisdom and the benefit of their miss-takes. I am happy with my own age as it is exactly the age I am. I allow my mind to be whatever age it chooses.

Hierarchy

There is no one who is better or worse than me. We are all equal in God's eyes. Therefore I do not envy others or think of myself as superior. The circumstance of my life where given to me as an opportunity to grow my soul. This is my individual path to do with it as I will. It is but a short time I am privileged to walk the Earth. I will use it wisely.

Soul Path

Earth is a classroom. People learn by
experience. Although I respect the wisdom
of others I know that my soul path is
 individual. I am here to learn lessons of
Courage, Tolerance, Self-Protection,
Self-Love, Ego, Love of Humanity and God-
Love. I know that God, my guides, angels
and my soul Self have mapped out the
challenges to help me grow. I know that I
may have to learn some things through
 ;reat difficulty. I accept this.

Acceptance

When I understand that I am fully
responsible for my thoughts and choices I
accept that I am a work in progress. I may
not always get it. I acknowledge that many
of my difficulties are consequences of my
own choices. If I change my patterns and
thoughts my circumstances will change.
God will guide me but will never remove
my ability to choose the easy way or the
hard way.

Love

I am loved. I am loved unconditionally by God and the universe who will wait patiently until I fully understand what this means.
I love myself unconditionally and will also wait patiently through good days and bad days recognizing that nothing is so terrible that it can't be changed. The life I want is but a thought and prayer away.
I surrender.

Ten Things I love About Myself:

1.
2.
3.
4.
5.
6.
7.
8.
9.
10.

Deborah Herman is an Intuitive Energy Artist who uses her automatic drawings for healing work and to assist people in connecting to their Divine Spark.

We are proud to include Deborah Herman as one of our Soul Odyssey authors. For more information about Deborah and our other offerings please sign up for our list at www.soulodysseybooks.com

Soul Odyssey Books is a division of Micro Publishing Media, Inc